SUCCESS BY DESIGN

A BLUEPRINT FOR ENTREPRENEURS WITH
FAITH & PURPOSE

CHE COX

TABLE OF CONTENTS

Prologue		5
Chapter 1:	The Hardships of Entrepreneurship	7
Chapter 2:	Building a Strong Foundation	15
Chapter 3:	Crafting Your Business Plan – Setting the Foundation for Success	23
Chapter 4:	Leadership, Relationships, and Building Your Support Network	33
Chapter 5:	Embracing Challenges and Overcoming Adversity	43
Chapter 6:	Staying Humble and Open to Guidance	51
Chapter 7:	Building a Legacy, Not Just a Business	61
Chapter 8:	The Bible – The Best-Selling Book of All Time	69
Bonus Material		77

PROLOGUE

In the beginning, every dream feels impossible. The vision is often blurry, the road unclear, and the challenges seem insurmountable. But for those who dare to dream—who not only dream but plan, and who not only plan but take action—there lies the potential to bring those visions to life. This is a book for the visionary, the one who sees beyond the now, who is willing to take the leap of faith, and who believes in something greater than what's in front of them.

Entrepreneurship is not for the faint of heart. It demands more than ideas; it requires action, persistence, and the courage to face obstacles head-on. There will be failures, and there will be moments of doubt, but these are the very fires that refine you.

In this journey, it is not enough to believe in yourself alone. The greatest entrepreneurs are those who align their dreams with something bigger—God's plan, God's purpose. Success, at its deepest level, is not just about financial gain. True success is about fulfilling a purpose, serving others, and building something that lasts.

This book is your guide to navigate the hardships of entrepreneurship with your faith as your foundation. It is filled with practical steps, biblical wisdom, and real-life experiences to help you create not just a business, but a legacy. The road will be hard, but every step will count.

Whether you are just beginning or already on your entrepreneurial journey, you are not alone. Your vision is a gift, and this is the blueprint to turn that vision into reality. Trust the process. Believe in your vision. And most of all, trust in the One who gave it to you.

CHAPTER 1:
The Hardships of Entrepreneurship

Introduction: Facing the Realities of Entrepreneurship

Starting a business is often seen through a lens of excitement, creativity, and financial freedom. Yet, few people talk about the difficult and overwhelming challenges that entrepreneurs face. While the potential rewards are great, the road to success is paved with uncertainty, failure, and moments of doubt.

Many entrepreneurs are forced to juggle countless roles—from marketing to finances to customer service—often without the comfort of a safety net. For every story of success, there are countless tales of long nights, empty bank accounts, and near failure. In this chapter, we will look at these realities, not to discourage you, but to prepare you for the path ahead.

Entrepreneurship is not about avoiding challenges but learning how to overcome them with resilience, belief, and a vision that carries you through the hardest times.

My Personal Journey: The Spark of Entrepreneurship

For me, the entrepreneurial journey began in an unexpected way—through a bead jewelry business which I started at the age of 16. What started as a simple creative outlet quickly became the catalyst for something much bigger. The process of crafting and selling bead jewelry gave me a taste of what it felt like to turn an idea into reality. It awakened a spark in me that I never knew existed. I was not just creating jewelry; I was creating possibilities.

That bead jewelry business was the beginning, but it was not without its challenges. There were setbacks, frustrations, and plenty of moments when I questioned whether I could do it. Yet, each obstacle strengthened my determination. Through the highs and lows, I realized something powerful: entrepreneurship is not just about the business—it is about the person you become in the process. It is about developing resilience and pushing past the barriers that stand in your way.

This realization has stayed with me through every business venture I have pursued since then. That is why, in this book, I will be sharing not only the practical steps to success but the mindset you need to adopt in order to overcome the hardships of entrepreneurship.

Belief in Vision, Self, and God

The most important part of entrepreneurship, which many do not realize, is belief. Not just belief in the business idea, but belief in your vision, yourself, and God. These are the foundational pillars that hold everything together.

1. Belief in Vision

Everything starts with a vision—an idea of what could be. But a vision is nothing without belief. You must believe in what you are trying to create. No one else will believe in it until you do. It is your vision that will carry you through the most difficult moments when everything seems like it is falling apart. That belief in your vision will push you to keep going, even when the odds are against you.

Key Point: Your vision is unique, and it is your responsibility to nurture and protect it. You must see the value in what you are building before anyone else can.

2. Belief in Yourself

It is not enough to believe in the vision; you must also believe in yourself. The hardships of entrepreneurship will test your confidence and force you to confront self-doubt. In those moments, you need to remind yourself of your capabilities and your worth. I have had moments of doubt when I questioned whether I had what it took to succeed. But it was my belief in myself that pushed me forward. With that belief, I was able to successfully scale our ATM business and, step into the world of clothing design, creating a brand that resonated with my vision. Both ventures grew from that unwavering confidence.

Key Point: Trust in your ability to grow, learn, and adapt. Failure is not the end; it is part of the process. Believing in yourself is the most critical factor in overcoming the challenges ahead.

3. Belief in God

As someone who has always valued my relationship with God, faith plays a vital role in entrepreneurship. There are times when things will not make sense, and you will wonder why certain doors are closing. In those moments, trusting in God's plan becomes essential. His guidance and wisdom can give you strength when you feel weakest.

The Bible teaches us about perseverance, resilience, and faith, all of which are qualities that every entrepreneur must develop. Your belief in God can ground you and keep you aligned with a greater purpose.

Key Point: Aligning your business goals with biblical principles can guide your journey. God's truth often leads us to deeper success when we trust in His timing and guidance.

Conclusion: Preparing for the Journey Ahead

Entrepreneurship is not just about building a business; it's about building yourself. The hardships you face will shape you in ways you never imagined. But by staying true to your vision, believing in yourself, and trusting in God, you can overcome the obstacles that lie ahead.

As you move forward in this book, you will learn the practical tools needed to succeed but remember that entrepreneurship starts with belief. Belief that you can create something from nothing, and that, no matter how tough it gets, you have what it takes to make your vision a reality.

Chapter 1 Worksheet:
Reflecting on Your Vision, Self, and God

1. Your Vision

    - What is your entrepreneurial vision? Describe it in detail. What do you want to create or achieve through your business?

        Answer: _____

        _____

    - How confident are you in this vision? Rate your belief on a scale of 1 to 10 and explain why you chose this number.

        Answer: _____

        _____

2. Belief in Yourself

    - What are your greatest strengths that will help you succeed as an entrepreneur?

        Answer: _____

        _____

    - What are your areas of self-doubt or weaknesses? List them and think about how you can work on improving them.

Answer: _____

_____

- Write down a moment in your life where you faced a hardship and overcame it. How did you manage to push through? How can you apply this to your entrepreneurial journey?

    Answer: _____

    _____

3. Belief in God

- How does your relationship with God guide your decision-making as an entrepreneur?

    Answer: _____

    _____

- What Bible verse or principle inspires you most when it comes to perseverance and entrepreneurship? Why?

    Answer: _____

    _____

4. Your Action Plan

- Based on what you have reflected on, write down three actions you can take this week to strengthen your belief in your vision, yourself, and your faith.

1: _____

2: _____

3: _____

1. Reflection Questions:

    - What has been your biggest challenge in entrepreneurship so far?

    - How has your faith influenced your ability to overcome hardships?

    - Think of a time when a challenge in your business taught you a valuable lesson. What was it, and how can you apply it going forward?

2. Assignment:

    - Write about a recent challenge: Take a journal and reflect on the biggest challenge you have faced in your business recently. Write down how you overcame it or how you plan to overcome it. Then, list 3 ways your faith can help you approach future challenges.

    - Action Step: Identify one problem in your business that you have been avoiding. Write down 3 actionable steps to address it starting this week.

CHAPTER 2:
Building a Strong Foundation

Introduction: Laying the Groundwork for Success

Every successful business begins with a solid foundation. Just as a house needs a solid base to withstand storms, your entrepreneurial journey requires careful planning, consistency, and attention to the minute details that will help you thrive long-term. Without these foundational steps, even the best ideas can crumble when faced with challenges.

In this chapter, we will cover how to build a firm foundation for your business, focusing on key areas such as creating a clear plan, maintaining discipline, and managing resources effectively. By the end, you will be ready to set strong roots that can support the growth and success of your business.

1. Crafting a Clear Business Plan

Your business plan is the roadmap for your entrepreneurial journey. It provides direction and ensures that you stay focused on your goals. A well-crafted plan should answer the following questions:

- What is your mission?

- Who is your target market?

- What problem are you solving?

- How will you generate revenue?

By answering these questions, you can define your path and keep your efforts aligned with your vision.

Key Point: Your business plan should be flexible but detailed enough to guide you through each stage of development. Remember, planning is about preparing for success.

2. Consistency is Key

Consistency is one of the most important habits for any entrepreneur. It is not enough to have bursts of inspiration; you need to show up daily. Whether it is reaching out to potential clients, creating content, or developing your product, consistency will separate you from the competition.

Entrepreneurs often lose momentum when they do not see immediate results, but persistence is what leads to breakthroughs.

Key Point: Set a daily routine that includes consistent actions toward your business goals. Small, steady steps will compound into considerable progress over time.

3. Managing Resources Wisely

A business is only as successful as its ability to manage resources effectively. This includes money, time, and human capital. Start by being clear about your priorities and understanding where to allocate your resources for the best return on investment.

Whether you are bootstrapping your business or securing outside funding, good financial management is crucial. Create a budget and stick to it, knowing when to invest and when to conserve resources.

Key Point: Do not be afraid to start small and grow slowly. Manage your resources with discipline, and you will ensure that your business remains sustainable in the long term.

Conclusion: Building for the Future

Building a strong foundation may seem tedious at times, but it is the key to ensuring long-term success. By crafting a clear plan, maintaining consistent effort, and managing your resources well, you are setting yourself up for growth and stability. Remember, businesses that thrive are built on solid ground, not on flashes of brilliance.

As you move forward, keep these foundational principles in mind, knowing that they will anchor your success in the years to come.

**Chapter 2 Worksheet:
Strengthening Your Foundation**

1. Crafting Your Business Plan

    - Write down your business mission in one sentence. What problem are you solving, and for whom?

        Answer: _____

        _____

    - Who is your target market? Be as specific as possible. (Age, gender, location, interests, etc.)

        Answer: _____

        _____

    - What is your strategy for generating revenue? Describe your main product or service and how it will make money.

        Answer: _____

        _____

2. Consistency

    - What actions can you commit to doing daily that will help you grow your business? List three habits you can start today.

1: _____

2: _____

3: _____

- How will you keep yourself accountable to these daily habits?

    Answer: _____

    _____

3. Managing Resources

- Write down your current business budget. Where are you giving the most resources, and are these allocations aligned with your priorities?

    Answer: _____

    _____

- What steps can you take to better manage your financial resources or time to maximize results?

    Answer: _____

    _____

4. Action Plan

- Based on your reflections, write three actionable steps you will take this week to build a stronger foundation for your business.

    1: _____

    2: _____

    3: _____

1. Reflection Questions:

- What does "belief in your vision" mean to you? How do you think God fits into your vision for success?

- In what ways has self-doubt hindered your progress in the past? How can you replace self-doubt with faith in God's plan?

- How would you define success in a way that aligns with both your business goals and your faith?

2. Assignment:

- Create a Vision Statement: Write a clear and concise vision statement for your business. This should include not only your business goals but also how your faith drives your entrepreneurial journey.

- Action Step: Write down one limiting belief you have been holding about yourself or your business. Replace it with a faith-based affirmation that you will use to overcome this belief (e.g., "I am capable because God has equipped me for this journey.").

CHAPTER 3:
Crafting Your Business Plan – Setting the Foundation for Success

Introduction: The Blueprint for Success

A successful business starts with a well-crafted plan. This is the blueprint that not only defines what your business will do but also how it will operate, grow, and serve its customers. In this chapter, we will explore how to craft a business plan that serves as the foundation for your entrepreneurial journey, ensuring that every move you make is purposeful and aligned with your vision.

A business plan is not just a document—it is a strategy. It is a way of thinking that guides your decisions, helps you anticipate challenges, and ensures that you stay on track even when things get tough.

1. Defining Your Mission and Vision

Every great business is built on a keen sense of purpose. Defining your mission and vision is the first step in your business plan because it sets the tone for everything else. Your mission is what your business will accomplish, while your vision is what success looks like for you and your customers.

Biblical Principle: Vision and Purpose

In Proverbs 29:18 (NIV), it says, *"Where there is no vision, the people perish."* This highlights the importance of having a clear, God-inspired vision for your business. As you build your plan, make sure that your mission aligns with your long-term goals and honors God's purpose for you.

Key Point: Start your plan by defining why your business exists and what difference it will make in the world.

2. Outlining Your Goals and Objectives

Once your mission and vision are clear, it is time to set specific goals and objectives. Goals are the big-picture outcomes you want to achieve, while objectives are the smaller, actionable steps that will help you get there.

SMART Goals: Make sure your goals are Specific, Measurable, Achievable, Relevant, and Time-bound. Setting SMART goals allows you to track your progress and stay focused.

Biblical Principle: Planning for Success

In Luke 14:28, Jesus asks, *"Suppose one of you wants to build a tower. Won't you first sit down and estimate the cost to see if you have enough money to complete it?"* This teaches us that careful planning and goal setting are vital for success. Planning with diligence ensures that you do not start a project you cannot finish.

Key Point: Write down specific, actionable goals that align with your mission and provide a clear roadmap for the next 1-5 years.

3. Understanding Your Market

Knowing your target audience and understanding the market is a key part of a successful business plan. You need to know who your ideal customers are, what they need, and how your product or service can solve their problems. This section of your business plan should include:

- Target Demographic: Age, gender, location, income level, and interests.

- Market Research: Who are your competitors, and what do they offer?

- Customer Pain Points: What problems do your customers face, and how will your business solve them?

Biblical Principle: Knowing Your Field

Proverbs 24:27 (NIV) says, *"Put your outdoor work in order and get your fields ready; after that, build your house."* This can be applied to knowing your market. Before launching your business, ensure you have a deep understanding of the field you are entering.

Key Point: Your business plan should show a clear understanding of the market, ensuring that your product or service meets the real needs of your customers.

4. Creating a Marketing and Sales Strategy

A great product means nothing if no one knows about it. Your business plan should outline how you plan to market and sell your product or service. This includes identifying the platforms you will use (social media, paid ads, email marketing, etc.) and the key messages that will attract your audience.

Biblical Principle: Spreading the Word

In Matthew 28:19 (NIV), Jesus commanded his disciples to *"go and make disciples of all nations."* Similarly, as an entrepreneur, you must "go out" and share the message of your business with the world. Effective marketing is about reaching people with the right message in the right way.

Key Point: Your marketing plan should clearly define how you will spread the word, attract customers, and ultimately drive sales.

5. Financial Projections and Management

Every good business plan includes financial projections. This section should detail your startup costs, revenue forecasts, profit margins, and cash flow expectations. It will help you decide how much capital you need and when you can expect to break even or make a profit.

Biblical Principle: Stewardship

1 Corinthians 4:2 (NIV) reminds us, *"Now it is required that those who have been given a trust must prove faithful."* As an entrepreneur, managing your finances with wisdom and

faithfulness is crucial. God calls us to be good stewards of the resources He provides.

Key Point: A financial plan helps you anticipate challenges and ensures that you are managing resources in a way that honors God and positions your business for success.

Conclusion: Building a Solid Foundation

Crafting your business plan is more than just filling out a document—it's about setting the foundation for your business's future. With a clear mission, defined goals, understanding of your market, a solid marketing strategy, and careful financial planning, you can move forward with confidence.

Just as the best chance for success comes when plans are aligned with truth, aligning your business plans with God's truth ensures a solid foundation that is built to last.

Chapter 3 Worksheet: Crafting Your Business Plan

1. Mission and Vision

- What is your business's mission? Why does your business exist?

    Answer: _____

    _____

- What is your vision for the next 5 years? What does success look like for you and your customers?

    Answer: _____

    _____

2. Goals and Objectives

- Write down three SMART goals for your business (Specific, Measurable, Achievable, Relevant, Time-bound).

    1: _____

    2: _____

    3: _____

- What is the first objective you need to achieve to reach each goal? Be specific.

    Answer: _____

    _____

3. Understanding Your Market

- Who is your target audience? Describe their age, gender, location, and key interests.

    Answer: _____

    _____

- What are the pain points your customers face? How will your business solve these problems?

    Answer: _____

    _____

4. Marketing Strategy

- What platforms will you use to market your business (e.g., social media, email, ads)? List two and explain why they are the best fit.

    Answer: _____

    _____

- What is the core message of your business? How will you present it to attract your audience?

    Answer: _____

    _____

5. Financial Planning

- What are your projected startup costs? How much capital will you need to get started?

    Answer: _____

    _____

- What is your revenue goal for the first year? When do you expect to break even or make a profit?

    Answer: _____

    _____

6. Action Plan

    - Based on your reflections, write three action steps you will take this week to improve your business plan.

        1: _____

        2: _____

        3: _____

1. Reflection Questions:

    - What is the most important part of your business plan, and how does it reflect your faith?

    - How does the principle, "The best chance for success comes when plans are aligned with truth," apply to your business strategy?

    - Have you included God's purpose for your life in your business planning? How can you ensure your plan aligns with His vision?

2. Assignment:

    - Business Plan Draft: If you have not already, draft the first 3 sections of your business plan (mission, vision, and goals). Make sure to align them with your spiritual values.

CHAPTER 4:
Leadership, Relationships, and Building Your Support Network

Introduction: The Power of Leadership and Relationships

Success in business is rarely achieved alone. Behind every great entrepreneur is a support network of advisors, mentors, partners, and team members who play a crucial role in helping the business thrive. In this chapter, we will explore the importance of building strong relationships and establishing yourself as a leader who others want to follow.

Leadership in business requires not just vision but also the ability to inspire, collaborate, and lift others up. The strength of your business will largely depend on the strength of your relationships—with employees, customers, partners, and even competitors. We will also discuss the importance of humility and remaining open to guidance, a key part of sustainable leadership.

1. Becoming a Servant Leader

Leadership in business is often misunderstood. Many see it as a position of power or authority, but true leadership is about service. Great leaders do not seek to dominate; they seek to lift others up and create an environment where people can flourish. This concept of servant leadership is vital for the long-term success of your business.

Biblical Principle: Leadership through Service

Jesus exemplified this in Matthew 20:26-28 (NIV) when He said, *"Whoever wants to become great among you must be your servant, and whoever wants to be first must be your slave—just as the Son of Man did not come to be served, but to serve, and to give his life as a ransom for many."* As an entrepreneur, your leadership should focus on serving your employees, customers, and partners.

Key Point: A great leader builds others up and creates an environment where everyone succeeds. By serving those around you, you establish trust and create a foundation of loyalty and respect.

2. The Importance of Humility and Openness to Guidance

One of the biggest pitfalls in entrepreneurship is overconfidence. Many business owners fall into the trap of thinking they know everything or that they don't need help. However, successful entrepreneurs know the value of humility and the importance of seeking guidance from others who have more experience.

Biblical Principle: King Nebuchadnezzar's Downfall

The Bible gives a powerful example of the dangers of overconfidence through the story of King Nebuchadnezzar in Daniel 4. Nebuchadnezzar's pride led to his downfall when he refused to acknowledge that his success came from God. He was humbled until he finally recognized God's sovereignty. This story serves as a reminder that even the most successful among us must remain humble and open to guidance.

Key Point: Stay humble, seek advice, and be open to learning from others. Overconfidence can be a stumbling block in your leadership and business journey.

3. Building Your Network: Mentors, Partners, and Advisors

No entrepreneur should walk the path alone. Whether you're just starting out or have been in business for years, surrounding yourself with a support network is crucial. This network should include:

- Mentors: People who have walked the path before you and can offer wisdom and guidance

- Business Partners: Trusted collaborators who share your vision and complement your skills.

- Advisors: Experts in specific areas (finance, marketing, operations) who can offer strategic advice to help you grow.

Each person in your network plays a different role, but together, they provide the support you need to overcome challenges and take your business to the next level.

Biblical Principle: The Counsel of Many

Proverbs 15:22 (NIV) reminds us that, *"Plans fail for lack of counsel, but with many advisers they succeed."* Building a strong network of advisors and mentors can help you see problems from different perspectives and provide insights that you may have missed.

Key Point: Your success in business is greatly influenced by the people you surround yourself with. Invest in building meaningful relationships with people who can offer wisdom, support, and encouragement.

4. Cultivating Relationships with Customers and Employees

Your relationships with your customers and employees are the lifeblood of your business. Happy employees lead to happy customers, and loyal customers drive the long-term success of your business. Cultivating these relationships requires genuine care, attention, and consistent effort.

Employee Relationships

As a leader, your job is to create a work environment where employees feel valued and supported. Happy employees are more productive, more loyal, and more invested in the success of the company. Lead with empathy and ensure that your employees feel heard and appreciated.

Customer Relationships

Your customers are the heart of your business. Building strong relationships with them requires more than just providing a good product or service—it's about creating a connection. Engage with your customers, listen to their feedback, and ensure they feel valued.

Biblical Principle: Loving Your Neighbor

In Matthew 22:39 (NIV), Jesus said, *"Love your neighbor as yourself."* This principle applies not just to our personal lives but to our business relationships. Treat your customers and employees with respect and care, and they will respond with loyalty and trust.

Key Point: Cultivate meaningful relationships with both your customers and employees. Their loyalty and engagement will drive your business forward.

Conclusion: Leading with Humility and Building a Supportive Network

Leadership and relationships are foundational elements in any successful business. By leading through service, remaining humble, and building a strong support network, you can create a thriving environment where your business, employees, and customers all succeed together.

Remember, leadership is about more than just making decisions—it's about empowering those around you to grow and succeed. Surround yourself with mentors and advisors, stay humble, and never stop building meaningful connections.

Chapter 4 Worksheet: Leadership and Relationships

1. Becoming a Servant Leader

    - What does servant leadership look like in your business? Write down one way you can serve your employees, customers, or partners this week.

        Answer: _____

        _____

    - How do you ensure that your leadership style is uplifting others and not just focused on your own success?

        Answer: _____

        _____

2. Staying Humble

    - Reflect on a time when overconfidence may have negatively impacted your decisions. How can you approach similar situations with more humility in the future?

        Answer: _____

        _____

    - Write down two areas in your business where you could benefit from outside guidance or mentorship.

Answer: _____

_____

3. Building Your Network

- Who are the mentors, advisors, or partners that you rely on for support? List three people who have positively influenced your business journey.

    Answer: _____

    _____

- What steps can you take to build stronger relationships with potential mentors or advisors? Identify one person you would like to connect with in the next month.

    Answer: _____

    _____

4. Relationships with Customers and Employees

- How are you currently building relationships with your customers? What could you do to create a stronger connection?

    Answer: _____

    _____

- How can you create a more positive and supportive environment for your employees? Write down one action you can take this week.

    Answer: _____

    _____

5. Action Plan

- Based on your reflections, write three action steps you will take this week to improve your leadership and relationships.

    1: _____

    2: _____

    3: _____

Additions:

1. Reflection Questions:

- What seeds are you sowing today that will reap benefits in the future?

- How have you seen the principle of "sowing and reaping" play out in your personal or professional life?

- What does biblical patience mean to you, and how can you apply it to your business journey?

2. Assignment:

- Map Your Seeds: Identify three areas of your business where you're currently "sowing seeds" (efforts, investments, relationships). Write down a timeframe for when you expect to start reaping results.

- Action Step: List three specific ways you can practice patience while waiting for the results of your hard work. Commit to daily reflection on these areas.

CHAPTER 5:
Embracing Challenges and Overcoming Adversity

Introduction: The Reality of Setbacks

Every entrepreneur will face challenges and setbacks—it's a fact of the journey. Whether it's a financial struggle, a failed product launch, or unforeseen external circumstances, adversity is part of the business landscape. However, how you respond to these setbacks is what will define your success.

In this chapter, we'll explore how to embrace challenges, overcome adversity, and use these moments to grow both personally and professionally. We'll also discuss how faith can provide the strength you need when times are tough, and how persistence is often the key to breaking through difficult times.

1. The Entrepreneur's Path: Trials and Triumphs

Many entrepreneurs start with a clear vision of success, but they may not anticipate the bumps along the road. It's important to remember that setbacks are not failures—they are opportunities to learn, adapt, and grow stronger. The most successful entrepreneurs view obstacles not as roadblocks, but as stepping stones to greater success.

Biblical Principle: Rejoicing in Trials

James 1:2-3 (NIV) reminds us, *"Consider it pure joy, my brothers and sisters, whenever you face trials of many kinds, because you know that the testing of your faith produces perseverance."* Challenges will come, but they are meant to build our perseverance and deepen our faith.

Key Point: Trials are inevitable, but they provide an opportunity for growth. Embrace them, knowing that every challenge you face is shaping you into a stronger leader and entrepreneur.

2. Staying Grounded in Faith During Hard Times

One of the most powerful tools for overcoming adversity is faith. When faced with difficult circumstances, it's easy to feel discouraged and want to give up. However, trusting in God's plan and staying grounded in faith can provide peace and clarity, even in the most challenging situations.

Faith allows you to stay focused on the bigger picture, knowing that setbacks are temporary, and that with persistence, you will overcome them. During these moments, it's essential to rely on God's strength, knowing that you don't have to carry the burden alone.

Biblical Principle: Trusting God in the Storm

In Matthew 14:29-31, we read about Peter walking on water toward Jesus. When Peter's faith wavered, and he focused on the storm around him, he began to sink. But when he refocused on Jesus, he was lifted up. In the same way, when the storms of business come, keeping your eyes on God and trusting in His provision will help you rise above the challenges.

Key Point: Stay grounded in your faith during times of adversity. Trust that God is guiding you through the storm and that His strength will sustain you.

3. Developing Persistence and Resilience

Persistence is one of the most important qualities an entrepreneur can develop. The journey of building a business is not easy, and those who succeed are often the ones who refuse to give up, even when the odds seem stacked against them.

Resilience is the ability to bounce back from setbacks and keep moving forward. It's about maintaining hope and optimism, even when things don't go as planned. Developing resilience is key to long-term success, as it allows you to weather the ups and downs of entrepreneurship without losing focus.

Biblical Principle: Pressing On

Philippians 3:13-14 (NIV) says, *"Forgetting what is behind and straining toward what is ahead, I press on toward the goal to win the prize for which God has called me heavenward in Christ Jesus."* This scripture encourages us to keep pressing forward, no matter the obstacles, focusing on the goal ahead and trusting in God's ultimate plan.

Key Point: Persistence and resilience are essential to success. Keep moving forward, knowing that setbacks are temporary, and growth comes through perseverance.

4. Practical Steps for Overcoming Challenges

While faith and persistence are crucial, there are also practical steps you can take to overcome adversity and stay motivated during tough times. Here are some strategies to help you push through challenges:

1. Break the Challenge into Manageable Steps

Large problems can feel overwhelming. Break them down into smaller, actionable steps. Focus on solving one piece at a time, and slowly, the bigger problem will become more manageable.

2. Seek Help and Guidance

Don't be afraid to reach out for help when facing a challenge. Whether it's seeking advice from a mentor, getting financial support, or asking for prayer, remember that you don't have to face adversity alone.

3. Maintain a Positive Mindset

Mindset is everything. Challenges can either defeat you or make you stronger, depending on how you view them. Cultivate a mindset of growth, focusing on what you can learn from each situation and how you can use it to improve.

4. Take Time to Reflect

Take a step back from the problem and give yourself time to reflect. Sometimes, the solution is clearer when you take a moment to breathe and reassess the situation with fresh eyes.

5. Keep Your Long-Term Vision in Mind

When faced with immediate challenges, it's easy to lose sight of the long-term vision. Keep your eyes on your goals and remind yourself why you started in the first place. Use your vision as a source of motivation when times get tough.

Conclusion: Victory in Adversity

Adversity is an inevitable part of the entrepreneurial journey, but it doesn't have to derail your progress. By embracing challenges, staying grounded in faith, and developing resilience, you can turn setbacks into opportunities for growth. Remember that the most successful entrepreneurs are not the ones who avoid challenges, but the ones who persevere through them with confidence, faith, and persistence.

Chapter 5 Worksheet: Embracing Challenges and Developing Persistence

1. Reflecting on Past Challenges

    - Think about a challenge you've faced in your business or personal life. How did you respond, and what did you learn from the experience?

        Answer: _____

        _____

    - How could you have approached that challenge differently, with more faith or persistence?

        Answer: _____

        _____

2. Staying Grounded in Faith

    - What are the biggest challenges you are currently facing in your business? Write them down and reflect on how you can trust God's guidance in overcoming them.

        Answer: _____

        _____

    - How can you strengthen your faith in this season of adversity? Is there a specific Bible verse or prayer that encourages you?

Answer: _____

_____

3. Developing Persistence

- What does resilience look like for you? List three qualities or habits that you believe will help you develop greater persistence.

    1: _____

    2: _____

    3: _____

- Write down a specific goal you are working toward and the challenges you anticipate. What practical steps can you take to stay persistent in achieving that goal?

    Answer: _____

    _____

4. Practical Steps for Overcoming Challenges

- Choose one current challenge in your business. Break it down into three smaller, actionable steps that you can take to start overcoming it.

    Step 1: _____

    Step 2: _____

Step 3: _____

5. Action Plan

- Based on your reflections, write three action steps you will take this week to face challenges with persistence and faith.

1:

2:

3:

1. Reflection Questions:

- Who has been a mentor to you, either in life or business? How have they impacted your journey?

- How do you seek guidance and learning from others? Are there areas in your life where you need more mentorship?

- In what ways can you be a mentor to someone else?

2. Assignment:

- Mentor Outreach: Identify one person you admire in business or life who could potentially mentor you. Craft an email or message to reach out and seek their guidance.

- Action Step: Identify one person you can mentor. Write down 3 ways you can support their growth over the next month.

CHAPTER 6:

Staying Humble and Open to Guidance

Introduction: The Dangers of Overconfidence

Success in business can sometimes lead to overconfidence. After reaching a certain level of achievement, it's easy to assume that you have all the answers, or that you don't need input from others. However, overconfidence can be a dangerous trap for entrepreneurs, leading to poor decisions, broken relationships, and even business failure.

In this chapter, we'll explore the importance of maintaining humility and remaining open to guidance, no matter how successful you become. We will also look at biblical examples of leaders who thrived by staying humble and those who fell because of pride. Finally, we'll discuss how accountability and continual learning are key to long-term success.

1. Humility as the Foundation for Success

Humility is not weakness; it is a strength that allows you to remain teachable and open to growth. As an entrepreneur, humility is critical because it keeps you grounded, ensures you're listening to your team and customers, and helps you avoid the pitfalls of pride.

Humility doesn't mean downplaying your achievements—it means recognizing that success is often the result of collective effort, and that there's always more to learn. A humble entrepreneur can acknowledge their strengths while also recognizing the contributions of others and the need for further development.

Biblical Principle: Pride Leads to a Fall

Proverbs 16:18 (NIV) warns, *"Pride goes before destruction, a haughty spirit before a fall."* Throughout the Bible, pride is seen as a dangerous trait that often leads to downfall. Humility, on the other hand, is a characteristic that leads to favor, wisdom, and greater opportunities.

Key Point: Stay humble, even in success. Recognize that there is always more to learn, and that true leadership comes from a place of humility and service.

2. King Nebuchadnezzar's Story: A Warning Against Pride

One of the most powerful biblical examples of the dangers of pride is the story of King Nebuchadnezzar. In Daniel 4, we learn that Nebuchadnezzar's pride in his accomplishments led him to believe that his kingdom was built by his own power. He failed to acknowledge that his success was given by God.

As a result, Nebuchadnezzar was humbled in a dramatic way—he lost his kingdom and lived like an animal for seven years, until he finally recognized God's sovereignty. Only when Nebuchadnezzar acknowledged that his success came from God was his sanity restored, and he was able to return to his throne.

This story serves as a powerful reminder for entrepreneurs: No matter how successful you become, pride can lead to downfall. Staying humble and giving credit where it's due—whether to God, your team, or others—is essential for maintaining long-term success.

Key Point: Always acknowledge the sources of your success, and be mindful of the dangers of pride. Stay humble, and remain open to God's guidance.

3. The Role of Accountability

Accountability is a key aspect of staying humble. Surrounding yourself with trusted advisors, mentors, or even a board of directors can help keep your ego in check and ensure that you are making decisions in the best interest of your business and its stakeholders.

Having people who can challenge you, offer different perspectives, and hold you accountable for your actions helps to prevent blind spots and ensures that you're constantly growing as a leader. Accountability isn't just about having others watch over you—it's about being willing to seek out advice and accept correction when needed.

Biblical Principle: Wisdom in Counsel

Proverbs 11:14 (NIV) says, *"For lack of guidance a nation falls, but victory is won through many advisers."* This emphasizes the importance of having wise counsel in your business journey. Having people you can rely on for advice and correction is crucial to staying on the right path.

Key Point: Build a network of accountability partners who can offer wisdom and hold you accountable for your decisions.

4. Remaining Open to Learning and Growth

The most successful entrepreneurs never stop learning. No matter how much success you've achieved, there is always room for growth, new knowledge, and fresh perspectives. Staying curious and continually seeking new skills ensures that you don't stagnate.

In the fast-paced world of business, change is constant. Whether it's learning new technologies, adapting to market trends, or improving leadership skills, being open to continual learning is essential for long-term success. Entrepreneurs who remain teachable are more likely to innovate, adapt, and stay ahead of the competition.

Biblical Principle: The Importance of Wisdom

Proverbs 9:9 (NIV) says, *"Instruct the wise and they will be wiser still; teach the righteous and they will add to their learning."* This reminds us that the pursuit of wisdom and knowledge is a lifelong journey. Staying open to instruction allows you to grow and make better decisions for your business.

Key Point: Stay curious, never stop learning, and remain open to new ideas and perspectives.

5. Embracing Constructive Criticism

One of the hardest parts of staying humble is being open to constructive criticism. No one enjoys hearing about their flaws or mistakes, but it's essential for growth. Constructive criticism allows you to see blind spots, improve your weaknesses, and make better decisions in the future.

As an entrepreneur, receiving feedback from customers, employees, and mentors is crucial for making necessary adjustments in your business. Rather than seeing criticism as an attack, embrace it as an opportunity to improve.

Key Point: Welcome constructive criticism as a tool for growth, and use it to refine your leadership and business strategy.

Conclusion: Staying Humble on the Path to Success

As you move forward in your entrepreneurial journey, staying humble and open to guidance is critical for sustained success. Whether it's maintaining accountability, seeking wise counsel, or continuing to learn and grow, humility ensures that you stay grounded, make better decisions, and honor the contributions of those around you.

Remember, success in business is not just about what you achieve—it's about how you achieve it. Humility will keep you on the right path, and with God's guidance, you can continue to grow and succeed in all aspects of your business and life.

Chapter 6 Worksheet: Staying Humble and Accountable

1. Reflecting on Humility

   - In what areas of your business do you struggle with pride? How can you practice humility in those areas?

     Answer: _____

     _____

   - What does humility look like in your day-to-day leadership? Write down one action you can take to lead with more humility this week.

     Answer: _____

     _____

2. Embracing Accountability

   - Who are the people in your life or business who hold you accountable? List their names and the roles they play in your accountability network.

     Answer: _____

     _____

   - How can you improve your accountability system? What steps can you take to ensure you're receiving honest feedback and counsel?

Answer: _____

_____

3. Remaining Open to Learning

- What new skills or knowledge areas do you need to learn to stay competitive in your business? Write down three things you want to learn in the next year.

    1: _____

    2: _____

    3: _____

- How will you seek out opportunities for learning and growth? List the resources, courses, or people you will reach out to.

    Answer: _____

    _____

4. Receiving Constructive Criticism

- Think about the last time you received constructive criticism. How did you respond, and what did you learn from it?

    Answer: _____

    _____

- How can you become more open to feedback and use it to grow in your business? Write down one way you can improve your ability to receive and act on constructive criticism.

    Answer: _____

    _____

5. Action Plan

    - Based on your reflections, write three action steps you will take this week to stay humble, remain accountable, and embrace learning.

        1: _____

        2: _____

        3: _____

Additions:

1. Reflection Questions:

    - In what areas of your life have you allowed overconfidence to cloud your judgment?

    - How do you remain open to instruction while maintaining confidence as a leader?

    - What lessons can you draw from the story of King Nebuchadnezzar about the importance of humility?

2. Assignment:

- Humility Inventory: Write down one area of your business where you've struggled with overconfidence or where you may have resisted outside advice. Then, list 2 actions you can take to open yourself up to guidance.

- Action Step: Ask a trusted colleague or mentor for feedback on a recent decision you've made in your business. Commit to applying their advice to your process.

CHAPTER 7:
Building a Legacy, Not Just a Business

As an entrepreneur, you've probably heard the phrase, "Build something that outlasts you." But what does that truly mean? In today's fast-paced world, many businesses focus solely on short-term profits. They aim to make money quickly without considering the long-term impact or how they'll leave a lasting imprint on the world. But true entrepreneurship is about more than just creating a business—it's about building a legacy.

A legacy isn't measured by how much money you've made or how popular your brand is in the moment. It's about the lasting effect your business has on people, communities, and even generations to come. It's about creating something of value that continues to impact lives long after you're gone.

1. The Importance of Long-Term Vision

Many entrepreneurs get caught up in the short game, focusing solely on quarterly profits or how they can grow their customer base right now. While these things are important, they are only part of the picture. If your focus is only on the here and now, you risk missing the bigger purpose of why you started your business in the first place.

When you shift your mindset to the long-term, you begin to think about sustainability. What systems can you put in place to ensure that your business thrives, even when you're no longer at the helm? How can you create value for your customers that keeps them loyal for years? Building a legacy means thinking about how your decisions today will shape the future of your business.

Take a look at successful companies that have stood the test of time. These businesses didn't just focus on profits; they focused on their mission, their values, and how they could continue to serve people. They made decisions with future generations in mind. Ask yourself: What will your business stand for decades from now?

2. Legacy Over Profit

Profit is a vital part of running a business, but it should never be your only goal. If your sole focus is on making money, you'll miss the chance to build something meaningful. True legacy builders know that the impact they have on others far outweighs financial success.

This doesn't mean you ignore profitability, but rather that you balance it with purpose. Businesses that build legacies focus on service—how they can improve the lives of their customers, communities, and employees. They ask themselves questions like:

- How can I use my business to make a difference in the world?

- What problems am I solving that will still matter years from now?

- How can I serve others while maintaining a successful business?

Think about how your business can leave a positive mark. Can you invest in community initiatives? Can you mentor future entrepreneurs or create opportunities for those who may not have access to resources? Your legacy is tied to the impact you make, not just the money you earn.

3. Faith-Based Legacy

For those of us who incorporate faith into our business practices, building a legacy takes on an even deeper meaning. We are called not just to succeed but to serve others and fulfill the purpose God has placed on our lives. Your business is an extension of that purpose.

Consider this: God gave you the vision for your business, and with that vision comes a responsibility to use your platform for something greater than yourself. It's an opportunity to glorify Him, serve others, and spread His values through your work. Whether you realize it or not, your business is a tool to fulfill His purpose in the world.

As you think about your legacy, ask yourself:

- Does my business reflect my faith?

- Am I building something that aligns with God's purpose for me?

- How can I use my business to positively impact others in a way that aligns with my spiritual values?

When your business is rooted in faith, the legacy you leave will extend far beyond profits or products. It will be a testament to God's work in your life and a reflection of His love and purpose.

4. Creating Sustainable Systems

A crucial part of building a legacy is creating systems that can sustain your business long-term. This includes everything from operational efficiency to financial planning. It's not enough to have a great idea; you need to ensure that your business can run smoothly, whether you're there or not.

Here are some practical steps to ensure your business is built to last:

- Standardize Operations: Document your processes so that anyone stepping into your role can easily understand how to run the business.

- Develop Key Leaders: Identify individuals who can carry on your vision and train them to take on leadership roles. Succession planning is vital to ensure your business's continued success.

- Diversify Revenue Streams: Don't rely on one product or service. Diversifying ensures that your business remains adaptable to changes in the market.

- Focus on Long-Term Customer Relationships: Build strong, lasting relationships with your customers by delivering consistent value and excellent service.

By building systems that can function independently of you, you are laying the groundwork for your business to thrive well into the future.

5. Preparing for Succession

Part of building a legacy is understanding that at some point, you will need to step aside. Whether you pass your business to a family member, a trusted employee, or sell it to new owners, it's important to have a succession plan in place.

A well-thought-out succession plan ensures that your business doesn't lose its direction or values once you're no longer in charge. Start thinking about this early, even if you're years away from stepping down. Who can continue your vision? How will the transition be managed?

Succession planning isn't just about choosing the right person; it's about ensuring they are prepared to lead. Invest time in mentoring your successor. Share your knowledge, values, and goals with them so they can carry on your vision with confidence.

6. Building a Legacy That Lasts

When you build a legacy, you're creating something that will continue to grow long after you're gone. This means investing not just in your business but in people, communities, and causes that matter to you. It means focusing on the bigger picture—how you can make a lasting difference.

A legacy is built over time, through dedication, perseverance, and a clear vision. By staying focused on your values, aligning your business with your faith, and planning for the future, you are setting yourself up for success that goes beyond the financial and touches lives for generations.

Reflection Questions:

- How do you want to be remembered as a business leader?

- What can you do today to ensure your business impacts others positively in the future?

- What steps are you taking to prepare your business for the next generation of leaders?

In the end, your business is not just about you—it is about the people you serve, the lives you change, and the legacy you leave behind. Build it with purpose, and your influence will last far beyond your lifetime.

1. Reflection Questions:

- What kind of legacy do you want to leave through your business?

- How does the idea of building a business for future generations change how you approach daily decisions?

- In what ways does your faith influence the legacy you are building?

2. Assignment:

- Legacy Vision: Write down a 1–2-page vision of the legacy you want to leave behind. Include how your business can positively impact future generations.

- Action Step: Show one initiative (community project, mentorship program, etc.) that you can implement within your business to start building your legacy today.

CHAPTER 8:
The Bible – The Best-Selling Book of All Time

The Bible stands as the most widely distributed, most translated, and best-selling book in history. Whether you are a believer or not, its influence cannot be denied. But beyond its sheer reach, the Bible's wisdom and teachings have shaped countless lives, societies, and even businesses. From world leaders to everyday people, many have turned to its pages not just for spiritual guidance but for practical principles that apply to life, leadership, and success.

1. A Timeless Guide

What makes the Bible so powerful? Its wisdom is timeless. It has stood the test of thousands of years, and yet, the principles it teaches are just as relevant today as they were when they were first written. The Bible addresses every aspect of human life—relationships, leadership, integrity, humility, and perseverance. It serves as both a moral compass and a practical guide for living.

For entrepreneurs, the Bible provides a foundation of values that can guide business decisions, interactions with others, and long-term vision. When we take biblical principles seriously, they shape not only how we run our businesses but how we live our lives.

2. Influence Beyond Religion

It is important to understand that the Bible's impact stretches beyond religious circles. Even people who may not believe in God have turned to the Bible for its profound insights into human nature and life principles. Leaders in fields as diverse as law, philosophy, business, and literature have drawn inspiration from its pages.

The Bible has influenced countless laws, governmental systems, and cultural practices around the world. In fact, many of the values that people respect in business today—like fairness, honesty, and treating others with respect—are rooted in biblical teachings. The Golden Rule, "Do unto others as you would have them do unto you," (Luke 6:31) is a cornerstone of ethical behavior in both personal and professional relationships.

3. Wisdom for Business and Leadership

The Bible offers profound insights into leadership and business practices. Take Proverbs, for example, which is filled with principles that are directly applicable to entrepreneurship:

- Proverbs 16:3 (ESV): "Commit your work to the Lord, and your plans will be established."

- Proverbs 11:1 (ESV): "A false balance is an abomination to the Lord, but a just weight is his delight."

Both verses reflect timeless truths that apply to how we conduct business. When we commit our work to God and act with integrity, we position ourselves for lasting success. The Bible teaches that honesty, diligence, and humility are the keys to sustainable leadership.

Similarly, Ecclesiastes teaches us about the importance of balance in life. While business is important, the Bible reminds us not to lose sight of our purpose, relationships, and faith in the pursuit of success. Building a business on biblical principles helps entrepreneurs keep the bigger picture in mind, ensuring that their legacy is one of integrity, not just profit.

4. The Bible's Practical Financial Wisdom

Many people overlook the fact that the Bible holds substantial teachings on finances, stewardship, and generosity. For example, Proverbs 22:7 warns about the dangers of debt: "The rich rule over the poor, and the borrower is slave to the lender." This timeless advice encourages entrepreneurs to avoid unnecessary debt and to be wise with financial decisions.

The Bible also teaches us the value of diligence and hard work. Proverbs 13:4 says, "The soul of the sluggard craves and gets nothing, while the soul of the diligent is richly supplied." This principle directly applies to entrepreneurship—success doesn't come from laziness but from consistent effort and dedication.

Generosity is another key theme in the Bible. Luke 6:38 (ESV) says, "Give, and it will be given to you." This principle of giving applies not only to personal life but also to business. Entrepreneurs who are generous with their time, knowledge, and resources often build stronger, more resilient businesses because they invest in the success of others.

5. The Bible's Global Influence

The fact that the Bible is the best-selling book of all time underscores its influence across cultures, languages, and generations. It has been translated into over 3,000 languages and continues to reach new audiences each year. Its message is universal, crossing borders and societal divides.

For entrepreneurs, the global influence of the Bible serves as a reminder of the power of values-driven leadership. A business rooted in integrity, honesty, and service has the potential to grow beyond borders, just as the Bible's influence has transcended national and cultural boundaries. These timeless principles resonate with people no matter where they are from.

6. Applying Biblical Wisdom to Your Entrepreneurial Journey

As an entrepreneur, applying biblical wisdom to your business can serve as a guidepost for decision-making, leadership, and personal growth. Here are some practical ways to incorporate the Bible's teachings into your entrepreneurial journey:

- Commit your plans to God: Begin every business decision with prayer, seeking God's wisdom and guidance. Trust that when your plans align with His will, they will succeed.

- Practice integrity in all dealings: Honesty and fairness should be at the core of every business transaction. Building trust is crucial to long-term success.

- Avoid the trap of greed: The Bible teaches us to be content and avoid the pursuit of wealth for its own sake. Focus on the impact you're making, not just financial gain.

- Be diligent and persistent: Just as the Bible praises hard work, your business requires consistent effort. Stay dedicated to your goals, even when faced with challenges.

- Give back: Whether through charitable giving, mentoring, or providing opportunities for others, use your business as a platform to give generously. This will not only build goodwill but also reflect the heart of God's teachings.

7. The Bible as the Blueprint

As you continue on your entrepreneurial journey, let the Bible be your blueprint for success. Its wisdom is timeless, its influence unmatched, and its principles invaluable. By aligning your business practices with biblical truths, you are building something far greater than just a profitable enterprise—you are creating a lasting legacy that reflects God's purpose for your life.

No other book in history has shaped as many lives, influenced as many leaders, or guided as many entrepreneurs as the Bible. Whether you are seeking practical advice, spiritual growth, or timeless wisdom, the Bible provides a foundation that cannot be shaken. In your hands is the blueprint for both personal and professional success.

Reflection Questions:

- How can you incorporate biblical principles into your daily business operations?

- In what ways can the Bible's teachings on finances and stewardship influence your business decisions?

- How does the Bible's global influence inspire you to think bigger and reach further with your business?

Conclusion: Moving Forward with Purpose, Vision, and Faith

As you close this book and reflect on the journey ahead, remember that entrepreneurship is not just about creating a business—it's about crafting a legacy. You now have the tools, principles, and steps to move forward, but the true success of your journey lies in action. It's not enough to dream or plan; it's the daily steps you take that will bring your vision to life.

Faith is your foundation. Your belief in yourself, your vision, and God's purpose will guide you through the highs and lows of business. Trust that the challenges you face are opportunities for growth, and know that perseverance will lead you to success, even when the road is difficult.

Aligning your purpose with God's truth has been the central theme of this book. When your plans are rooted in this foundation, you are not only working toward financial or personal success but also building something that honors Him. Continue to seek wisdom, humility, and guidance from others, while maintaining your boldness in the vision you've been given.

This is only the beginning. The principles, strategies, and insights in this book are meant to equip you for the journey ahead, but they will only work if you put them into practice. Take the time to reflect on where you are now, envision where you want to be, and commit to taking action every day.

Entrepreneurship is not an easy path, but it's a rewarding one for those who remain faithful, focused, and fearless. Your legacy awaits—now go and build it.

BONUS MATERIAL

Step-by-Step Guide to Forming an LLC Without a Service

Forming an LLC on your own is completely doable if you follow the proper steps. Here's how to do it without paying for an external service:

Step 1: Choose Your State of Formation

- Website: Visit your state's Secretary of State website (each state has its own).

- For example, if you're forming an LLC in California, go to the California Secretary of State website: https://www.sos.ca.gov/business-programs.

- If you're forming in Texas, use the Texas Secretary of State website: https://www.sos.state.tx.us/corp/.

- Find your state's business formation section. Most states will have a section called "Start a Business" or "Form an LLC."

- Click on the section for LLC formation instructions and locate the forms you'll need to file the Articles of Organization (sometimes called Certificate of Formation).

Step 2: Choose and Register Your LLC Name

- Use your state's business name search tool to ensure your desired LLC name is available. You can typically find this tool on the state's Secretary of State website under "Business Name Availability."

- The name should include "LLC" or "Limited Liability Company" to comply with state rules (e.g., "YourBusinessName LLC").

Example Search Links:

- California Name Search: https://businesssearch.sos.ca.gov

- Texas Name Search: https://direct.sos.state.tx.us/acct/acct-login.asp

Step 3: Appoint a Registered Agent

- A registered agent is someone (or a company) designated to receive legal documents for your LLC. The registered agent must have a physical address in the state where your LLC is formed.

- If you are forming the LLC in your home state, you can be your own registered agent.

- If you need help, you can hire a registered agent service, which usually costs around $100-$300 annually.

Step 4: File the Articles of Organization

- Go to your state's Secretary of State website and find the form for Articles of Organization or Certificate of Formation.

- Most states allow you to file online, but some still require paper forms to be mailed.

- You will need to provide:

- LLC name

- Registered agent's name and address

- LLC's principal office address

- LLC purpose (can be a general business purpose)

- Pay the required filing fee, which ranges from $50 to $500 depending on the state.

Example Filing Pages:

- California LLC Filing: https://llcbizfile.sos.ca.gov

- Texas LLC Filing: https://www.sos.state.tx.us/corp/forms_boc.shtml

- Pro Tip: Most states have online filing portals to make this faster, but you can also print and mail the form if preferred.

Step 5: Draft an LLC Operating Agreement

- An Operating Agreement outlines how your LLC will operate, including ownership percentages, member responsibilities, and profit distribution. This is not always required by law, but it's highly recommended.

- For single-member LLCs, the Operating Agreement defines how you'll handle your business's finances and management.

- You can draft one yourself using templates found online, or consult a lawyer for a customized version.

Pro Tip: Some state websites may have Operating Agreement templates available to download, or you can find them on sites like www.RocketLawyer.com , www.lawdepot.com or www.Nolo.com

Step 6: Obtain an EIN (Employer Identification Number)

- An EIN (Employer Identification Number) is needed for tax purposes, hiring employees, and opening a business bank account.

- Go to the IRS website: https://www.irs.gov/businesses/small-businesses-self-employed/apply-for-an-employer-identification-number-ein-online

- The process is free and takes just a few minutes online.

- Pro Tip: Even if you don't plan to hire employees, getting an EIN is important for separating your business finances from personal finances.

Step 7: File for Necessary Business Licenses and Permits

- Depending on your business type and location, you may need to obtain local licenses or permits to legally operate.

- Check with your city, county, or state websites to find out what licenses your business needs. Common licenses include health permits, zoning permits, or professional licenses.

Example Links:

- California: https://www.calgold.ca.gov/

- Texas: https://www.texas.gov/business

Step 8: Register for State Taxes (if applicable)

- Depending on your state, your LLC may need to register for state taxes, such as sales tax, income tax, or unemployment tax (if you hire employees).

- Visit your state's Department of Revenue or tax office to register.

Example Links:

- California Sales Tax Registration: https://www.cdtfa.ca.gov

- Texas Comptroller (for tax registration): https://comptroller.texas.gov/taxes

Step 9: File Annual Reports and Pay LLC Fees

- Many states require LLCs to file annual reports or biennial reports to keep the business in good standing. These reports are often due on the anniversary of your LLC formation and come with a small fee.

- Check your state's LLC maintenance rules to ensure you file on time and avoid penalties.

Example Links:

- California LLC Annual Report: https://bizfileonline.sos.ca.gov

- Texas LLC Maintenance: https://comptroller.texas.gov/taxes/franchise/

Summary Checklist for DIY LLC Formation:

1. Choose your state and visit the Secretary of State website.

2. Select and register a unique LLC name.

3. Appoint a registered agent (yourself or a third party).

4. File Articles of Organization online or by mail.

5. Draft an Operating Agreement for internal use.

6. Obtain an EIN from the IRS for free.

7. Apply for any required licenses or permits at the state or local level.

8. Register for state taxes (if applicable).

9. File annual reports and pay any LLC fees.

Using an LLC Formation Service (like www.bizee.com)

LLC formation services like Bizee, LegalZoom, or ZenBusiness allow you to form an LLC in just a few simple steps, saving you time and effort. Here's how to do it:

Step-by-Step Guide Using an LLC Formation Service:

1. Choose Your LLC Formation Service

- Visit the website of the service you've chosen (www.bizee.com, www.LegalZoom.com , www.ZenBusiness.com etc.).

- Most services have pricing tiers (basic, premium, etc.). Select the package that fits your needs. Basic packages usually cover the essentials, while premium packages might offer extras like EIN registration or registered agent services.

- Pro Tip: Compare pricing and features across different services. www.Bizee.com and www.ZenBusiness.com are known for being affordable, while LegalZoom might offer more personalized options at a higher price.

2. Input Your LLC Information

- Once you've selected a package, the service will prompt you to enter your business information:

- Your LLC's name

- State of formation

- Business purpose

- Your personal details (as the LLC owner or manager)

- The service typically does a name availability search for you, ensuring the LLC name isn't taken.

- Pro Tip: Choose a name that reflects your business and is easy to market. Services like www.Bizee.com will also check if your business name is available for website domains.

3. Choose Additional Features (if needed)

- These services usually offer optional add-ons, such as:

- EIN registration (so you don't have to apply through the IRS separately)

- Operating Agreement templates

- Registered Agent services (useful if you don't want to handle this yourself)

- Compliance reminders (helpful for annual reports or state filing requirements)

- Pro Tip: If you're not familiar with legal or tax filings, opt for a service that includes an EIN and Operating Agreement in their packages to simplify your process.

4. Let the Service Handle the Filing

- Once you've filled in all the required information and chosen any add-ons, the service will take care of filing the Articles of Organization with the Secretary of State in your chosen state.

- Depending on the state, this process can take anywhere from a few days to several weeks. Many services offer expedited filing for an extra fee.

- Pro Tip: You can track the status of your filing through the LLC service's dashboard.

5. Receive Your LLC Documents

- After your LLC is successfully formed, the service will send you the official LLC documents, which typically include:

- Articles of Organization

- Certificate of Formation (or equivalent document)

- Operating Agreement (if requested)

- Some services offer digital storage, so your documents are saved online for easy access.

- Pro Tip: Once you receive your documents, open a business bank account using the provided LLC formation paperwork.

6. Ongoing Services (Compliance and Maintenance)

- Many LLC formation services offer ongoing compliance support. They'll send you reminders for state filings like annual reports or franchise taxes, ensuring you don't miss important deadlines.

- If you opted for a Registered Agent service, they'll continue receiving official correspondence on your behalf.

- Pro Tip: Use these compliance reminders to avoid penalties and keep your LLC in good standing.

Advantages of Using an LLC Formation Service:

- Speed: Services like www.Bizee.com or www.ZenBusiness.com can complete the process in minutes, and they handle all the paperwork for you.

- Convenience: You don't need to navigate state websites or fill out complex forms. The service takes care of it.

- Extras: Many services offer helpful add-ons, such as EIN registration, Operating Agreement templates, or registered agent services, simplifying your life further.

Pricing Breakdown for Most Services (Estimated):

- Basic Package: $49 - $100 (includes filing LLC documents)

- Mid-Tier Package: $150 - $250 (includes EIN, operating agreement, and expedited filing)

- Premium Package: $300 - $500+ (includes registered agent services, compliance support, domain name registration)

Summary of Steps Using an LLC Formation Service:

1. Select an LLC formation service (www.bizee.com, www.ZenBusiness.com , www.LegalZoom.com etc.).

2. Input your business information and let the service handle the name availability search.

3. Choose any additional features (EIN, registered agent, etc.).

4. Pay for the service and let them file your Articles of Organization.

5. Receive your official LLC documents and use them to set up your business bank account.

6. Utilize ongoing compliance services to keep your LLC in good standing.

Assignment:

- Take Action: Based on the bonus materials, choose one legal action you need to take (e.g., file for an LLC, trademark a business name). Complete it within the next 30 days.

(IN ORDER FOR YOUR VISION TO BECOME REALITY, YOU NEED TO TAKE ACTION ON EVERYTHING LEARNT. DO NOT WALK AWAY AND JUST SAY "THAT WAS A GREAT BOOK", APPLY WHAT YOU HAVE LEARNT AND MOVE AGGRESSIVELY TO THE LIFE THAT YOU ENVISION).

Here is a list of Secretary of State (or equivalent) websites for each U.S. state. These sites allow you to form an LLC, file documents, and access business resources.

Secretary of State Websites by State:

1. Alabama
   https://www.sos.alabama.gov

2. Alaska
   https://www.commerce.alaska.gov/web/cbpl/

3. Arizona
   https://www.azsos.gov

4. Arkansas
   https://www.sos.arkansas.gov

5. California
   https://www.sos.ca.gov/business-programs

6. Colorado
   https://www.sos.state.co.us

7. Connecticut
   https://portal.ct.gov/sots

8. Delaware
   https://corp.delaware.gov

9. Florida
   https://dos.myflorida.com/sunbiz

10. Georgia
https://sos.ga.gov

11. Hawaii
https://cca.hawaii.gov/breg

12. Idaho
https://sosbiz.idaho.gov

13. Illinois
https://www.cyberdriveillinois.com

14. Indiana
https://www.in.gov/sos

15. Iowa
https://sos.iowa.gov

16. Kansas
https://sos.ks.gov

17. Kentucky
https://sos.ky.gov

18. Louisiana
https://www.sos.la.gov

19. Maine
https://www.maine.gov/sos

20. Maryland
https://egov.maryland.gov/businessexpress

21. Massachusetts
    https://www.sec.state.ma.us/cor

22. Michigan
    https://www.michigan.gov/sos

23. Minnesota
    https://www.sos.state.mn.us

24. Mississippi
    https://www.sos.ms.gov

25. Missouri
    https://www.sos.mo.gov

26. Montana
    https://sosmt.gov

27. Nebraska
    https://sos.nebraska.gov

28. Nevada
    https://www.nvsos.gov

29. New Hampshire
    https://sos.nh.gov

30. New Jersey
    https://www.nj.gov/state

31. New Mexico
    https://www.sos.state.nm.us

32. New York
   https://www.dos.ny.gov/corps

33. North Carolina
   https://www.sosnc.gov

34. North Dakota
   https://sos.nd.gov

35. Ohio
   https://www.sos.state.oh.us

36. Oklahoma
   https://www.sos.ok.gov

37. Oregon
   https://sos.oregon.gov

38. Pennsylvania
   https://www.dos.pa.gov

39. Rhode Island
   https://sos.ri.gov

40. South Carolina
   https://www.sos.sc.gov

41. South Dakota
   https://sdsos.gov

42. Tennessee
   https://sos.tn.gov

43. Texas
https://www.sos.state.tx.us

44. Utah
https://corporations.utah.gov

45. Vermont
https://sos.vermont.gov

46. Virginia
https://scc.virginia.gov

47. Washington
https://www.sos.wa.gov/corps

48. West Virginia
https://sos.wv.gov

49. Wisconsin
https://www.wdfi.org/corporations

50. Wyoming
https://sos.wyo.gov

ICING ON THE CAKE!!

EXTRA Bonus Material:
Trademarks, Registration, and Step-by-Step Guide

This section covers the essential steps and procedures for trademarking or patenting your business idea or product in the United States.

Trademark Registration Process:

1. Preliminary Steps:

- Search Existing Trademarks: Before filing, use the Trademark Electronic Search System (TESS) on the www.uspto.gov (United States Patent and Trademark Office) website to check if a similar trademark already exists

- Decide on the Type of Trademark: Will it be for a word, logo, or symbol? Decide whether you're trademarking a name, slogan, or design.

2. Application Preparation:

- Description of Goods/Services: Clearly describe the products or services associated with the trademark.

- Choose the Filing Basis:

- Use in Commerce: If you're already using the trademark in business.

- Intent-to-Use: If you plan to use the trademark but haven't yet.

3. Filing the Application:

- Visit the USPTO website and access the Trademark Electronic Application System (TEAS) to file your application.

- Fees: Filing fees range from $250 to $350 per class of goods or services.

4. Examination by the USPTO:

- A USPTO attorney will review your application to ensure it meets legal requirements. This process can take several months.

5. Publication for Opposition:

- If the examining attorney approves the application, it will be published in the Official Gazette for a 30-day opposition period. During this time, others can challenge the registration.

6. Registration:

- If there's no opposition or if it's successfully resolved, your trademark will be registered, and you'll receive a registration certificate.

7. Maintaining Your Trademark:

- Between the 5th and 6th year: You must file a Declaration of Continued Use.

- Every 10 years: You must file for renewal to keep your trademark active.

Checklist for Trademark Registration:

- Conduct a comprehensive search to ensure the trademark is available.
- Determine the type of mark (word, logo, or symbol).
- Decide on the class of goods or services to file under.
- Prepare the application through the USPTO TEAS system.
- Pay the appropriate fees.
- Monitor your application status for USPTO approval or opposition.
- File for renewal between the 5th-6th and 10th years.

Patent Registration Process:

1. Conduct a Patent Search:

- Use the USPTO Patent Full-Text and Image Database (PatFT) to search for any existing patents related to your invention.
- Alternatively, consider hiring a patent attorney or agent for a professional patent search.

2. Determine the Type of Patent:

- Utility Patent: For new and useful inventions (machines, processes, compositions of matter).

- Design Patent: For new, original, and ornamental designs.

- Plant Patent: For new plant varieties.

3. Prepare the Patent Application:

- Provisional Application: This is a preliminary application that allows you to secure a filing date without a formal patent claim. It gives you a year to file a full application.

- Non-Provisional Application: A full patent application with detailed claims, drawings, and specifications of the invention.

4. File the Application:

- Submit the patent application through the USPTO EFS-Web (Electronic Filing System). Ensure the application is thorough and includes detailed drawings, descriptions, and claims.

5. Examination by the USPTO:

- The USPTO will assign a patent examiner to review your application, which can take anywhere from 18-36 months, depending on the complexity and backlog.

6. Patent Issuance:

- If your application is approved, you'll receive a patent grant, which gives you exclusive rights to your invention for up to 20 years from the filing date (for utility patents).

7. Maintenance Fees:

- For utility patents, you need to pay maintenance fees at 3.5 years, 7.5 years, and 11.5 years to keep the patent in force.

Checklist for Patent Registration:

- Conduct a thorough patent search.

- Determine the type of patent (utility, design, or plant).

- Decide whether to file a provisional or non-provisional application.

- Prepare detailed drawings and descriptions of the invention.

- File the patent application with the USPTO.

- Monitor the status and respond to any USPTO office actions.

- Pay maintenance fees at required intervals for utility patents.

Thank You

Dear Reader,

Thank you, from the depths of my heart, for choosing to invest your time, mind, and spirit into *"Success by Design: A Blueprint for Entrepreneurs with Faith & Purpose."* It's an honor to be part of your journey, and I pray that the words in these pages will serve as a guiding light, helping you achieve the success you envision—not just for yourself, but for the greater purpose that God has designed for your life.

I believe that every step we take as entrepreneurs is not just a pursuit of wealth or recognition, but a pursuit of the calling that God has placed within us. I've written this book with the hope that it will inspire you to see your business ventures not only as a means of financial success, but as a mission to glorify Him and serve others.

As you navigate the path of entrepreneurship, remember these words from the Bible:
"Commit to the Lord whatever you do, and He will establish your plans." — Proverbs 16:3 (NIV)

Know that when your vision is aligned with God's truth, your potential is limitless. I encourage you to keep faith at the center of your work, and trust that He is with you every step of the way—especially when the road is difficult.

Thank you for allowing me to share this journey with you. May this book empower you to take bold steps of faith, as you build not only a business, but a legacy of purpose and impact.

With heartfelt gratitude,
Che Cox

www.ingramcontent.com/pod-product-compliance
Lightning Source LLC
Chambersburg PA
CBHW052332220526
45472CB00001B/388